FROG RESCUE

FROG RESCUE

Changing the Future for Endangered Wildlife

GARRY HAMILTON

FIREFLY BOOKS

A FIREFLY BOOK

Published by Firefly Books Ltd. 2004

First printing

Publisher Cataloging-in-Publication Data (U.S.)
Hamilton, Garry.
Frog rescue : changing the future for endangered wildlife / Garry Hamilton. —1st ed.
[64] p. : col. photos. ; cm. (Firefly animal rescue)
Includes index.
Summary: Provides details and facts about frogs from around the world, their endangerment and extinction, and a range of conservation programs to save them. Includes profiles of individual conservationists and frog species.
ISBN 1-55297-597-5
ISBN 1-55297-596-7 (pbk.)
1. Frogs — Juvenile literature. 2. Endangered species — Juvenile literature. I.Title. II. Series.
597.86 21   QL737.C23.H36 2004

Library and Archives Canada Cataloguing in Publication
Hamilton, Garry, 1962-
Frog rescue : changing the future for endangered wildlife / Garry Hamilton.
(Firefly animal rescue)
Includes index.
ISBN 1-55297-597-5 (bound).— ISBN 1-55297-596-7 (pbk.)
1. Frogs—Juvenile literature. 2. Endangered species—Juvenile literature.
3. Wildlife conservation—Juvenile literature. I. Title. II. Series.
QL668.E2H34 2004   j597.8'9   C2004-903042-6

Published in the United States in 2004 by
Firefly Books (U.S.) Inc.
P.O. Box 1338, Ellicott Station
Buffalo, New York 14205

Published in Canada in 2004 by
Firefly Books Ltd.
66 Leek Crescent
Richmond Hill, Ontario L4B 1H1

Design: Ingrid Paulson
Maps: Roberta Cooke

Printed in Singapore

The Publisher acknowledges the financial support of the Government of Canada through the Book Publishing Industry Development Program for its publishing activities.

TABLE OF CONTENTS

IT'S A FROG'S LIFE

Frogs are amazingly diverse. You can find them in tropical rain forests, north of the Arctic Circle, high in the Himalaya Mountains and in many of the world's driest deserts.

They've also been around a lot longer than you might think. Frogs first appeared at least 190 million years ago, when Earth was still dominated by dinosaurs. Their ancestors were the first large animals to live on dry land. Today, there are close to 5,000 known frog species, and the list continues to grow as scientists probe deeper into the remote corners of the planet. Together with salamanders and caecilians (worm-like creatures that live mainly underground), they are amphibians—animals that live part of their lives in water and part on land.

But frogs are in trouble. Fewer than 30 years ago, herpetologists—scientists who study amphibians and reptiles—began to notice that frogs were disappearing from areas where they once thrived. By 1989, amphibians were in dramatic decline all over the world, and it wasn't just in areas crowded with people. Many species were disappearing from the remote wilderness as well. "Until that point, I don't think anybody realized that it was anything other than a local problem," says one veteran biologist.

Different species face different threats. The destruction of their habitat, overharvesting by humans, competition from other species and deadly diseases cause local problems. Pollution, climate change and increased radiation from the sun may be making matters worse on a global scale. Some 32 frog species are now thought to have died out since the early 1970s, and another 25 are classified as "missing in action"—they're either extinct, or so rare that scientists haven't been able to find them. Almost a hundred others are critically endangered.

While these lists are likely to grow, there is hope. During the past decade, researchers have been working together and sharing information on frog declines. They're learning more about what's killing the frogs—and what needs to be done to save them.

Frogs are found on every continent except Antarctica,
although the vast majority live in tropical regions.

THE STORY SO FAR

1974 Australian scientists discover the extraordinary gastric brooding frogs, which rear their young in their stomachs. By the mid-1980s, both species of this frog would mysteriously disappear from the wild.

1987 India, one of the leading exporters of frog legs to Europe, stops the trade because of its ecological impact. That same year, poison dart frogs are protected under the Convention on International Trade in Endangered Species (CITES).

∧ A researcher monitors artificial breeding structures for poison dart frogs in the Peruvian rain forest.

1989 Scientists meet at the First World Congress of Herpetology in Canterbury, England, where they acknowledge for the first time that amphibians are experiencing a worldwide decline.

1991 Scientists form the Declining Amphibian Populations Task Force, an international group that now includes some 3,000 frog experts.

1993 The Amphibian Research Centre, one of the world's only institutions dedicated entirely to frog conservation, opens near Melbourne, Australia.

1995 Students in Minnesota find the first of many frogs with extra legs, missing eyes and other deformities.

1996 A herpetologist in Panama discovers frogs dying from what is later identified as a chytrid fungus. It would soon be named as the culprit in many other troubled frog species.

1998 Scientists report that mass frog deaths in northeastern Australia and Central America are likely the result of the chytrid fungus.

1999 The Kihansi spray toad—a rare species that lives only in a single Tanzanian gorge—is threatened with extinction by a new hydroelectric dam.

Dainty and surreal, a poison dart frog from Costa Rica shows off its splendor.

2000 Biologist Rainer Schulte forms a group to protect poison dart frogs in the rain forests of Peru.

2001 In an effort to protect endangered frogs, the California Department of Fish and Game reduces its practice of stocking lakes with trout.

2002 Some 400 captive-bred Oregon spotted frogs—a species identified just five years earlier—are released into a marsh on the Seabird Island Indian Reserve in British Columbia.

2003 Bushfires in Australia's Kosciusko National Park rage through the last remaining habitat of the southern corroboree frog, setting conservation efforts back a decade or more.

MAKE YOURSELF AT HOME

All frogs require water and land, but different species satisfy these needs in different ways. This is one big reason why they're so diverse.

As tadpoles, many species are perfectly happy in any body of fresh water they can find, even human-made ones like cattle-watering tanks or dam basins. Other species are choosier, and depend on ponds, streams, swamps or lakes. They may also find homes in temporary pools or puddles formed by melting snow or seasonal rains. Tadpoles of many tropical species live in small pockets of water that get trapped in rain-forest plants called bromeliads. In North America, some frogs begin their lives in mud pools created by large mammals, or ponds formed by beaver dams. As adults, frogs live on the forest floor, on sand dunes, in the canopies of trees, on rocky cliffs or in caves.

∧ A strawberry poison dart frog's life begins in this bromeliad bath, high in the rain forest canopy.

Frogs often depend on conditions being just right—streams moving at a certain speed, or water that's a certain temperature or depth. Some frogs can't swim but still need to get their young to water. They depend on plants or steep rocks overlooking creeks, placing their eggs on them so that newly hatched tadpoles fall safely into the water below. Others need the warmth of hollow logs to survive the winter.

Sometimes these needs are so specialized that an entire species is confined to a tiny area—perhaps a single mountainside or watershed. These frogs are often of particular concern to conservationists because a single event—a drought, or a change in the landscape by humans—can be a disaster. The species may have nowhere else to go.

< Because roads often divide different frog habitats, tunnels like this—widely used in Europe since the 1960s and more recently in North America—help protect frogs from vehicles during their annual migrations.

UNDER MY SKIN

Frogs are sensitive to their environment, and one reason is their remarkable skin. Unlike other animals protected by scales, feathers, hair or thick hide, amphibians have a delicate outer membrane that allows them to absorb moisture from the air and breathe in oxygen. But it also means that they're like a sponge when it comes to pollutants.

Frogs are even more vulnerable early in life. Unlike those of birds or reptiles, amphibian eggs have no protective shells—just a thin, jellylike bubble. Chemicals and pollutants can easily pass through and threaten the developing tadpole inside.

Living both in water and on land, frogs depend on two food chains, two environments

In addition, simply by being amphibious, frogs are exposed to more threats than most other animals. Relying on both water and land means that they depend on two food chains and two environments. Trouble in either one is trouble for them.

Many frogs cannot tolerate the effects of acid rain. Eggs can be killed or damaged by too much ultraviolet (UV) radiation from the sun. And many frogs are sensitive to pesticides, fertilizers and industrial pollutants. All of these substances may be threatening frogs in the wild, but it's difficult for scientists to pinpoint their individual effects. Most studies have focused on fish or other species with more commercial value than the humble frog.

But frog researchers would like to see this change. To them, the frog's sensitive nature makes it a perfect barometer of the health of the environment.

Looking more alien than amphibian, the fully limbed froglet of a Costa Rican rain frog gets ready for life in a new world.   >

For the Kihansi spray toad, the world is a small place—very small. Discovered in 1996, these tiny golden-brown toads live only along a steep, 3-mile (5 km) stretch of the Kihansi River in Tanzania, East Africa. Their habitat is just a few grassy areas that are continuously showered with mist from two large waterfalls.

∧ A sprinkler system maintains artificial habitat in the Kihansi Gorge.

At least that was the situation before December 1999, when authorities flipped the switch on a brand new hydroelectric dam. The project provided a poor nation with much-needed energy, but it also disrupted the flow of the river. Water that normally plummeted through the gorge was diverted into turbines, and the vital waterfalls were reduced to tiny trickles. Without the crashing water, much of the habitat created by the mist began to dry up. Only a few months after the dam began operating, 93 percent of the spray habitat was lost.

This, of course, was bad news for the toads. They depend on certain insects found only in the spray zones. They also have thin skins that require constant moisture, but lack the ability to swim—without their tiny, unique environment, they cannot survive.

What followed was one of the most dramatic—not to mention unusual— amphibian rescue attempts ever made. In September 2000, engineers installed pipes and sprinklers near one of the former waterfalls, hoping to mimic the spray generated by the falling water. Half-a-year later, the built a larger system upstream near the second waterfall. Five hundred spray toads were also sent to zoos in the United States, where they became part of a captive-breeding program.

Discovered only in 1996, the Kihansi spray toad is in dire trouble.

At first, it appeared to be working. By May 2003, there were some 12,000 toads in the larger spray zone, up from a low of 1,300. But then disaster struck. By July, researchers discovered the spray toad numbers had collapsed again. A few months later, the news was even worse. "Despite intensive searching during the day and night, we did not find any toads in any of the spray wetlands where the species is known to occur," reported Ché Weldon, an herpetologist at North West University in Potchefstroom, South Africa.

Weldon and others suspect disease is to blame, and they now fear the worst. They had hoped that hibernating toads would emerge during the rainy season, but surveys in 2004 again came up empty. "The majority of workers are hesitant to say that the spray toads are extinct in the wild," says Weldon, "but we have very little hope left of finding live toads."

David Wake shakes his head as he talks about how frogs have fallen so far, so fast.

"We've got fossil amphibians from 160 million years ago that look exactly like living ones today," says Wake, a professor at the University of California at Berkeley. "To think that organisms like that would be disappearing during our lifetimes—our puny, short lifetimes, relative to 160 million years—is incredible to me."

If one person has played the key role in alerting the world to this sad situation, it's Wake, who is now one of the world's most respected amphibian biologists. In the 1980s, he started hearing about local frog declines from many scientists. "So many people were talking about it," he recalls. In 1989, he chaired a meeting in England that drew scientists from all over the world, and they suddenly realized they were facing a global problem.

For Wake, education is the first step. He and several graduate students launched AmphibiaWeb, a Web site that's collecting profiles of every single amphibian species known to science. He also started Froglog, a newsletter that brings together reports on frog declines and other news from all over the world.

∧ Looking astonishingly familiar, a 49-million-year-old fossilized frog is an ominous reminder of what's being lost.

David Wake eyes a bromeliad, a favorite hangout for many rain forest frogs.

"I've always felt we would be most effective if everybody could simply see the problem," he says. "Then they would rise to the occasion. I think that's the most effective way of getting things done in the world." Certainly this approach seems to explain why scientists have rallied around the plight of amphibians. The true test now will be whether it will also spur the public.

> "Like it or not, humans are running this planet now. And it's on our watch that amphibians are checking out. I think we all ought to be very concerned about that."

19

FUNGUS AMONG US

The gathering of the golden toads in Costa Rica, first witnessed in 1972, was one of nature's splendid spectacles. Every year, hordes of brightly colored *Bufo periglenes* would mate in temporary pools surrounded by rain forest. At the largest breeding site, scientists reported seeing up to 1,500 frogs at a time.

Then the species vanished. In 1989, only a few toads turned up at the main gathering site. Since then, not one has been seen anywhere.

What could have caused such devastation? The likely answer did not emerge until the late 1990s, when scientists investigated similar mass die-offs in Australia and Panama. They discovered that the animals were dying from a microscopic fungus called chytrid (pronounced *KIT-rid*).

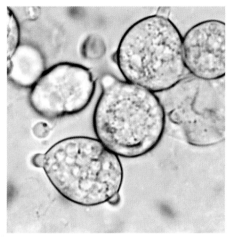

∧ Looking little like the killers they are, spores of the chytrid fungus converge beneath a microscope.

Scientists now know that the chytrid fungus is the main culprit in many frog declines all over the world, dating back at least a quarter century. The fungus has been found on nearly 100 species from six continents. It's blamed for the extinction of not only the golden toads, but also at least half a dozen species in Australia alone. Entire populations have been wiped out within a few months, often in the remote wilderness.

There have been wildlife epidemics before, of course. A notorious virus swept through Africa in the 1890s, killing huge numbers of hoofed mammals such as wildebeests and antelopes. But even that disaster failed to wipe out an entire species, or spread to another continent. What's happening to frogs may be unprecedented, according to Australian disease expert Lee Berger, one of the first to identify the killer. "In the recorded history of the world, I don't think there is anything that compares."

< Mass congregations of male golden toads were a common sight in the cloud forests of Costa Rica until the species mysteriously disappeared after 1989.

Things were looking up for Australia's southern corroboree frog. After decades of slow decline, these distinctively colored critters had been given hope by a recovery program begun in 1997. Although just a few hundred individuals had remained, the release of more than 2,000 captive-raised tadpoles appeared to be helping.

Then came the bushfires. In the summer of 2003, the worst fires in the region's history burned through all known corroboree frog habitat. "We're pretty sure we lost a lot of frogs," says recovery team member Gerry Marantelli.

The disaster highlights the challenges involved in rescuing a vulnerable species, as well as the importance of acting quickly. If the recovery project hadn't got off the ground when it did, the fires may have put the species beyond saving.

Southern corroboree frogs are found only in Kosciusko National Park in southeastern Australia. Adults live among the leaf litter and other debris on the floor of snow-gum woodlands. In the summer, they venture to nearby bogs to mate and lay eggs in water-filled depressions that form in the moss that will later flood with the spring snow melt. Until the 1970s, the area teemed with corroboree frogs—up to 3 per square foot (30 per m²), by one account. By the mid-1980s, however, scientists knew the species was in trouble, and by 1997 the population was estimated at just 500 and falling.

∧ Severe drought is complicating corroboree frog recovery efforts in the Snowy Mountains of Australia.

< The southern corroboree frog, named after the Australian Aboriginal word for "gathering" because it was once so common, is now fighting for survival.

∧ An Australian wildlife expert examines precious corroboree frog eggs.

Nobody knew why. Because the frogs lived in a national park, they were largely protected from habitat destruction. Chytrid fungus had been found on some, but the population decline seemed too slow for an epidemic. Was the habitat drying up? Perhaps, but frogs continued to disappear even during years of abundant rain. The best guess was that disease had devastated the frogs at some point, making them so sensitive to such factors as drought that they were now unable to bounce back on their own.

The recovery team collected eggs and hatched them in captivity, where survival rates are around seven times higher than in the wild. They returned most of the tadpoles to their native habitat, keeping the rest for captive breeding. It's slow going: corroboree frogs lay only about 30 eggs a year, and once these hatch it's five years before they're ready to lay eggs of their own. Tragically, the fires struck just as many of the released tadpoles were reaching sexual maturity.

The fire brought other bad news, too. "There were areas that used to be wet, green sphagnum moss," says Marantelli. "Now there's an inch of ash and that's all." While patches of suitable habitat remain, full recovery will have to wait until the forests and bogs return, which will take years, if not decades. "It's tiring," admits Marantelli. "We knew this would be a long process when we started, and it's not looking any shorter. You're looking at another 20 years of trying to recover this species. It's a long haul."

Although not nearly as serene as a snow-gum woodland, the artificial breeding centers such as this one near Canberra may be the corroboree frog's last hope for survival.

All hope is not lost. In 2002, the first of the captive-born frogs were old enough to breed in captivity, which they did successfully. The younger captive frogs should be ready to produce offspring soon. Once some larger questions surrounding the species' survival are settled, the team should be ready to start returning the frogs to the wild. Adds Marantelli, "We're not giving up."

In 1991, several sharp-snouted torrent frog tadpoles were taken from a stream in northeastern Australia and shipped to Gerry Marantelli, a frog expert at Melbourne Zoo. By trying to breed them in captivity, Marantelli was part of a last-ditch effort to save a species in sharp decline. But little was known about the frogs, or why they were in such trouble. When the captured animals began to die, all Marantelli could do was watch. The species has not been seen since 1994, and is probably extinct.

"To watch a species go extinct is a very serious wake-up call."

"To know species are being eliminated from the wild is one thing," Marantelli says today. "But to watch it happen in front of you, and be powerless to do anything about it—that was a very serious wake-up call."

It was shortly after this that Marantelli quit his job to devote all his energy to saving frogs. In 1993, he started the Amphibian Research Centre (ARC), now the unofficial headquarters for frog conservation in Australia, a country with more threatened species than any other.

Through the ARC, Marantelli has helped to create an army of frog conservationists. He and his assistants visit some 20,000 students a year, introducing kids to the wonders of frogs and the threats they face. Under his guidance, dozens of schools are involved in restoring frog habitat, building new ponds and reintroducing frogs to their former ranges. They build breeding enclosures, design Web sites and raise money. Marantelli has also enlisted hundreds of volunteers to identify, count and monitor frog populations across his home state of Victoria. It was this effort that led to the recent discovery of six new populations of growling grass frogs, yet another endangered Australian species.

Gerry Marantelli is on a one-man mission to save Australia's vanishing frogs.

Marantelli earns praise from scientists around the world for his skill and dedication, but he hasn't forgotten the sharp-snouted torrent frog. It's a tragedy he never wants to see repeated. "I love these animals," he says. "They're remarkable creatures and I think the world would be a lot worse off without them."

THE FROG TRADE

In fairy tales, evil spells turn princes into frogs. An old wives' tale says that touching a toad will give you warts. In the Bible, frogs are one of the deadly plagues. But in reality, it's humans who have brought harm to frogs—in many different ways.

Perhaps most surprisingly, frogs were once used in North America for human pregnancy tests. A woman's urine sample was injected into a frog and, if pregnancy hormones were present, the frog would lay eggs. Widely used in the 1950s, the practice was abandoned as more modern tests were developed.

The same cannot be said for other forms of frog harvesting. Frogs are commonly used as sport-fishing bait in in the United States and Canada. Around the world, high-school students dissect frogs in biology class, and many scientists conduct lab experiments on them. In China, skins and other frog parts are thought to have medicinal properties—you can buy these products in drugstores and markets. In other countries, particularly France and Belgium, frogs' legs are a delicacy served in fine restaurants.

∧ For some, frogs are a delicacy.

Frogs are also popular pets, especially the poison dart frogs of Central and South America. These delicate, spectacularly patterned creatures are highly treasured in Europe, North America and Japan, with rare frogs selling for up to $500 (U.S.). Although it is illegal to take these animals from the wild except by permit, that doesn't stop unscrupulous collectors. In 2000, officials in Bogota, Colombia, arrested a smuggler with 300 frogs, including several rare species, worth an estimated $30,000 (U.S.). Law enforcement is spotty, though, and some believe that thousands of frogs are successfully smuggled every year.

< A favorite among frog collectors, poison dart frogs use bright colors to warn potential predators of the toxins that ooze from their backs. For centuries the Choco Indians of South America used these poisons to coat the tips of their blow darts.

In 1981, Rainer Schulte was exploring a small stream in a patch of undisturbed rain forest in Peru when he came across a poison dart frog with a remarkable appearance. The frog had a blue belly marbled with strings of black, a cherry-red back, and bright yellow racing stripes down each side. It was a species previously unknown to science. Schulte later named it *Epipedobates cainarachi*—the cainarachi poison frog.

∧ A recycled soft drink bottle is part of a novel attempt to save frog habitat in Peru.

Today, Schulte doesn't like visiting the site because it has been turned into cattle pastures and cornfields. His beloved frog is on the verge of extinction.

The sad tale highlights a major flaw in the protection of poison dart frogs: while it is illegal to trade in these highly prized animals except by special permit, very little is done to protect their habitat. "Without those habitats," says Schulte, "species will go extinct."

Since he began studying poison dart frogs in the early 1980s, Schulte has watched his rain forest shrink by more than half. His life is now dedicated to not only studying poison dart frogs, but to saving them.

A conservation group he founded in 2000 has produced manuals to help local authorities protect frogs and their habitat. It has helped to nab smugglers. It has teamed up with zoos in Europe to create emergency captive-breeding programs, for species afflicted by the deadly chytrid fungus.

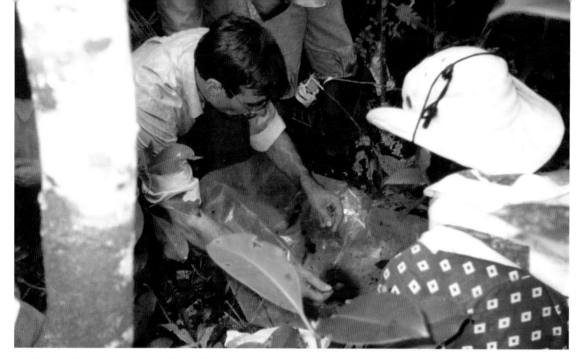

Deep in the Peruvian rain forest Rainer Schulte is training a legion of poison dart frog farmers.

Schulte's most ambitious scheme, however, is to show local farm workers (called *campesinos*) how to raise poison dart frogs in the wild, which helps them to earn money in a way that's both legal and sustainable. Many poison dart frogs lay their eggs on the leaves of bromeliads, plants with built-in cups for trapping rainwater. When the eggs hatch, the tadpoles fall into the water cups, where they live until they mature into frogs. Schulte has discovered that scattering bottom halves of plastic soft-drink bottles throughout the forest—to mimic bromeliads—encourages frogs to move in and breed, expanding the population.

His goal now is to help the *campesinos* profit from the worldwide demand for poison dart frogs. In the summer of 2003, the first group was waiting for permits to begin legally harvesting the excess poison dart frogs generated on 9,500 acres (3,800 ha) in central Peru. Similar projects are being developed in Ecuador and Colombia.

If all goes as planned, these will be the first steps in Schulte's plan to convince the world that a rain forest is worth more alive than dead.

Mirza Dikari Kusrini is trying to get her fellow Indonesians interested in frogs—and that's no small challenge. Frogs don't get a lot of attention in this country of 217 million people. There are only a handful of frog scientists, and almost no information on whether amphibians are declining. "We don't even know how many species we have," says Kusrini.

∧ The frog harvest means income for many Indonesians, but is it sustainable?

An ecology professor at Bogor Agricultural University on the island of Java, Kusrini has developed a program for teaching children about local frogs. She gives high-school students the rare opportunity to participate in field research. And she's one of the few—if not *only*—people investigating how the frog-leg harvest affects Indonesia's amphibian populations.

Indonesia is the leading supplier of frog legs to Europe. According to Kusrini, between 1990 and 2000, the country exported 4,000 tons (3.6 million kg) annually— a cargo that adds up to roughly 62 million frogs a year. No one knows whether the three species involved can survive such a harvest.

Kusrini first fell under the spell of these neglected creatures in 1998 after coming across a new book on Indonesian frogs—the first ever written by someone from her country. "Like most Indonesians, I always assumed there were only two or three kinds of frogs around us. Then I read there were 40 species on Java and Bali alone." Intrigued, she and a student conducted a frog survey on the Bogor campus. "To our surprise we found 14 species."

Indonesian high school students learn about the wonders of frogs.

Since then, she has been busy spreading the word in schools. "I started the program thinking we need to educate more people about frogs. And what better way to start than with children?" Her efforts appear to be paying off. When she needed two high-school students to help out on a recent three-day field trip, 50 applications landed on her desk. She ended up taking five volunteers.

"We have such a lot of biodiversity around us. We need to learn more about it before it disappears."

WHEN ALIENS ATTACK

You would think that life would be grand for the mountain yellow-legged frog. Native to the lakes of California's Sierra Nevada Mountains, this species lives in such cherished places as Yosemite National Park. In the early 1990s, however, mountain yellow-legged frogs were found in only 16 of the 86 areas where they were common decades earlier.

A large part of the problem can be summed up in a single word: trout.

When the glaciers receded from the Sierras some 10,000 years ago, they left behind fish-free lakes—ideal frog habitat. But for a century, people have been stocking these lakes with trout for sport fishing. Trout are greedy predators that eat large numbers of tadpoles, and where these bullies reside, mountain yellow-legged frogs are few and far between, or gone entirely.

Frogs often suffer when new species are introduced. For one thing, they're not well equipped for self-defense. Their eggs lack protective shells. Adults and tadpoles have no sharp claws, shells or other means of warding off attack. They can't even escape to safer territory very well— their bodies aren't made for fleeing great distances.

Some frogs do have strategies for avoiding becoming lunch, but these weapons often work only on age-old enemies. In eastern Australia, for instance, spotted tree frog tadpoles are poisonous to native fish. When the English arrived, however, they stocked the waterways with sport fish brought from Europe. These new fish don't mind the poison at all, and eat up the tadpoles like candy.

Rats hitchhiking aboard ships are thought to have helped drive some New Zealand frogs to extinction. Mosquito fish, introduced to many areas to help control mosquito larvae, and crayfish—accidentally released by sport fishermen who use them as bait—also eat tadpoles and eggs. Even other frogs can be a problem. Bullfrogs were brought to western North America by people hoping to raise them for food. Some escaped, however, and they now threaten many native species.

< Although a source of bliss for sport fishermen, the tranquil lakes of California's Sierra Nevada Mountains have become death traps for tadpoles preyed upon by introduced trout.

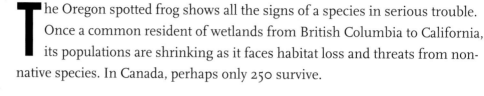
The Oregon spotted frog shows all the signs of a species in serious trouble. Once a common resident of wetlands from British Columbia to California, its populations are shrinking as it faces habitat loss and threats from non-native species. In Canada, perhaps only 250 survive.

^ An adult Oregon spotted frog, Canada's most endangered amphibian.

"Whenever you get low numbers like that, there is always a chance that some random event will just knock them all out," says John Richardson, an ecologist at the University of British Columbia in Vancouver.

Formed in 1999, the Oregon Spotted Frog Recovery Team faces a big challenge. Unlike most frogs, members of this shy species spend almost their entire lives in water, and most of their habitat has been drained for farming and other uses. What remains has been overrun by bullfrogs and green frogs introduced from eastern North America. Another problem is reed canary grass, a European plant that grows thicker than native vegetation and eliminates potential egg-laying sites. "Also, if they get into an area with reed canary grass, the frogs can't move effectively," says Richardson. "If a predator is chasing them, they don't have an escape route."

One of the recovery team's first efforts has been removing bullfrogs and reed canary grass, and transferring eggs from areas where they would likely die. Some eggs are hatched at the Vancouver Aquarium and the Greater Vancouver Zoo, where tadpoles are safe from predators. Froglets are later returned to their old homes.

The team is also creating new habitat. This is especially challenging, since scientists don't yet understand all of the spotted frog's quirky requirements. They have spent three years learning, though—several frogs were even fitted with small devices that emit radio signals, allowing researchers to track their every move.

An official from the Vancouver Aquarium releases young spotted frogs into a temporary holding pen, hopefully the first step towards building a new population in the wild.

Scientists now know that spotted frogs lay their eggs in very shallow water, no more than 2 to 4 inches (5 to 10 cm) deep. This water needs to be out of the shade of trees, as the sun's warmth speeds development of the eggs. The water level must also be stable, or the eggs risk drying out or being submerged too deeply. Once the tadpoles emerge, they too prefer shallow water, likely for protection from predators. Adult frogs, however, need deeper water.

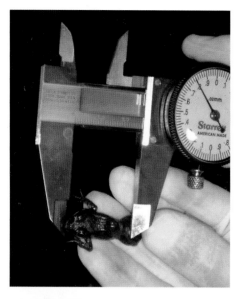

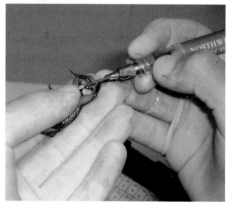

^ Leaving no detail unrecorded, researchers measure and tag spotted frogs before releasing them into the wild.

Not surprisingly, such habitat preferences match what used to exist near large rivers like the Fraser before flood control measures contained seasonal shifts in water levels.

The recovery team is now hoping to focus on more direct measures aimed at bringing the species back from the brink. In 2002, some 400 froglets were reintroduced into marshland on Seabird Island, one of the three remaining natural habitat sites. And by the summer of 2003 researchers were ready to begin conversion of a dry, empty field into what they hope will one day be almost 4 acres (1.5 ha) of brand new—and very wet—spotted frog habitat. It will take at least two years before suitable native vegetation is properly established in this new site, and several more years before introduced frogs will have reached breeding age. But for those scientists who will be watching closely, it will be well worth the wait. "This is a species where I think there is a lot of potential for recovery," says Richardson. "There is an optimism within our team that this really can be done."

HEAVYWEIGHT BOUT

Goliath frogs are the giants of the frog world. Reaching up to 12 inches (30 cm) and weighing up to 6½ pounds (3 kg), they are the largest frog species on the planet.

But these brutes are in trouble. Unlike the big bullfrogs of North America, which can eat almost anything and thrive almost anywhere, *Conraua goliath* lives only near fast-flowing rivers in the coastal regions of Cameroon and Equatorial Guinea in West Africa. Their range is so small partly because goliath frog tadpoles eat plants that grow only around certain waterfalls and rapids.

Until recently, this habitat was largely uninhabited by humans. Today, however, the clearing of rain forests and the damming of rivers are rapidly eroding this already tiny range. In addition, goliath frogs attract collectors, who sell them as pets, and are a source of food for local people, who consider them a delicacy.

There are currently no restrictions on the international trade of goliath frogs, but the species is now considered vulnerable. Fortunately the San Diego Zoo and the World Wildlife Fund have teamed up to save the goliath frog from extinction. Researchers are studying the habits of these giant amphibians, which until recently have remained largely unknown to science. In the future, they hope to find ways to preserve the goliath frog's dwindling habitat before it's too late.

∧ The Goliath frog of West Africa is a big frog with an increasingly small world.

39

MY, HOW YOU'VE CHANGED

All backboned animals experience change, but none as dramatically as frogs. In only a few short weeks, a creature adapted to underwater life that eats nothing but plants suddenly morphs into a meat eater perfectly at home on dry land. This small miracle is called metamorphosis.

On the surface, it's remarkable enough. Tadpoles begin to grow arms and legs. Their tails shorten. Skin grows over their gills. Underneath, it's nothing short of a complete renovation. Tadpoles lose their teeth, their jaws change shape, tongue muscles develop, connections between brain and body are rewired, cartilage is replaced with bone, intestines are remodeled to accommodate the new diet, ears develop, eyes move from the side of the head to the top, old blood cells are replaced with new ones better suited for processing oxygen, skin glands form, lungs grow—the list goes on and on.

∧ A bullfrog tadpole on the dramatic road to adulthood.

Metamorphosis is controlled by hormones, which travel throughout the body and tell cells how to behave—tail cells, for instance, are directed to commit suicide. These complex signals, though, can be easily disrupted. Tadpoles that are exposed to ultraviolet light, parasites, pesticides or herbicides often become deformed frogs. Indeed, frog metamorphosis has become a valuable lab tool for testing how chemicals affect cell development. If something interferes with a tadpole's ability to turn into a frog, there's a chance that it might also be dangerous to other animals—including humans.

< Limbless but not helpless, tadpoles of red-eyed leaf frogs peer up through their watery world.

THE CASE OF THE FIVE-LEGGED FROG

One day in August 1995, eight students and a teacher from a middle school in southern Minnesota set out on a field trip. It would be a day none of them will likely forget.

∧ Experts have been alarmed by a sharp rise in the number of deformed frogs, like this Oregon spotted frog with extra legs.

On a farm with a small pond, the students came upon a hideously deformed northern leopard frog. Then they found another. And another. By the time they were done, they had 22 frogs, half of them resembling something from a horror movie—some with twisted legs, others with extra limbs sprouting from the sides of their bodies.

Once the discovery hit the news, people began finding deformed frogs elsewhere. They've now been reported in 46 American states and four Canadian provinces, as well as in Japan, Europe and Australia.

Although some deformities are normal in the wild, the frequency at which they're now occurring is unnatural, especially in the western and midwestern U.S. In some areas, 90 percent of the frogs have been affected.

As scientists began investigating the mystery, they focused on two suspects: either UV radiation from the sun, or pesticides or other chemicals may have interfered with tadpole metamorphosis. But no one has been able to prove these theories.

Pieter Johnson, a young graduate student of zoology at the University of Wisconsin, was one of the scientists on the case. He had read about studies linking frog deformities to tiny, wormlike parasites called trematodes, which burrow into tadpoles and disrupt metamorphosis. Johnson put trematodes and tadpoles together in laboratory tanks, and then waited to see what happened. The results were shocking. In one tank, where tadpoles were exposed to a level of infection much lower than what they'd see in nature, every single frog that survived metamorphosis was deformed.

> "What struck me was the severity of the deformities," says Johnson. "It wasn't just an extra digit here, an extra digit there. This was real extreme. We would have five or six extra limbs, or animals with no hind limbs whatsoever." Johnson and his colleagues then surveyed a hundred sites in five western states. The researchers found that where deformities were common, there were almost always large numbers of trematodes.

But another mystery remains: why has the number of deformities risen so dramatically? Trematodes spend part of their life cycle inside snails, and snails thrive in areas with lots of algae. In turn, algae flourishes when livestock manure and fertilizer are washed into the water by rains. Adding all of this up, Johnson and others now believe that trematodes are on the rise due to modern farming practices.

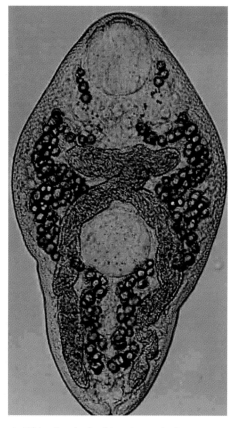

∧ This simple-looking trematode parasite is a prime suspect in the mystery of the deformed frogs.

43

With their life-threatening deformities, a pair of misshapen leopard frogs dramatically illustrates the severity of the crisis.

Pesticides or other chemicals may be playing a role as well. In one recent study, researchers found that pesticides alone did not cause deformities. However, frogs exposed to both pesticides *and* trematodes developed deformities far more commonly than those faced only with trematodes.

> Most deformed frogs are easy prey and cannot reproduce, and these factors can lead to the decimation of a whole population. Fortunately, says Johnson, the solution may be as easy as watching what goes into ponds. "People don't pay a lot of attention to ponds," he says. "But amphibians depend on them."

FROG OR TOAD?

What's the difference between a frog and a toad? The answer is not as straightforward as you might think.

Both belong to the order Anura, which separates them from the other amphibians —newts, salamanders and worm-like creatures known as caecilians. But there is no clear scientific distinction between frogs and toads, and technically all anurans are frogs.

That said, some species are classified as "true frogs" and others as "true toads." Generally, true toads (which make up the family Bufonidae, with more than 300 species, including cane toads) have rough, warty, dry skin and spend more time on land. Their legs are shorter and built for walking. They lay eggs attached to long strings, rather than in clusters. Their skin tends to be brownish rather than green or yellow, and they lack teeth.

True frogs (the family Ranidae, with some 400 species, including bullfrogs and northern leopard frogs) tend to have smooth, moist skin and spend more time in or near water. Their bodies and legs are thinner, longer and better adapted for swimming, jumping or, in some cases, climbing trees.

Beyond these two families, the distinction is blurry. Some species have warty skin but are called frogs, while some called toads look slimy. Other species have a mix of characteristics that could earn them either label. Perhaps the best rule is the one followed by the experts — when in doubt, call it a frog.

CREATIVE CAREGIVERS

In 1974, scientists discovered a frog so bizarre, some people thought it was a joke. Living in the rain forests of Queensland, Australia, the frogs swallowed their eggs and raised them in their stomachs. When the eggs hatched—releasing not tadpoles but up to 20 tiny froglets—the young animals climbed up their mother's throat and out her mouth.

Gastric brooding frogs, as they became known, were no joke. But they were perhaps the most unusual example of the ways that frogs can reproduce and look after their young.

Most frogs use a more familiar method: they lay their eggs in water and leave them to hatch into tadpoles, which eventually morph into small adults. But other frogs have evolved as variations on this theme. Many are what are known as direct developers—they lay eggs on land, and their young skip the tadpole stage, emerging from the eggs as froglets. Some frogs even give birth to live young.

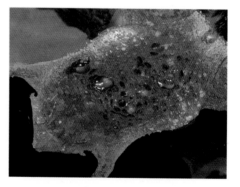

∧ The rather frightening looking Surinam toad hatches young beneath skin that forms over her eggs once they've been placed on her back.

Truly amazing is the way certain species get involved as parents. The strawberry poison dart frog lays eggs on land. Once these hatch, the mother deposits her tadpoles into water-filled bromeliads, which grow off the branches of rain-forest trees. There the mother feeds them with unfertilized eggs for some species, it's dad who tends the eggs until they hatch.

While fascinating, these reproductive habits make it hard for conservationists to save frogs, particularly when it comes to captive breeding. This was tragically illustrated as the gastric brooding frogs went into steep decline in the late 1970s and early 1980s. Nobody could figure out fast enough how to get them to breed in captivity—and they disappeared.

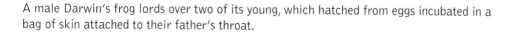
A male Darwin's frog lords over two of its young, which hatched from eggs incubated in a bag of skin attached to their father's throat.

For biologist Joan Mayol, it was a trip to remember. One evening in 1980, he hiked to a remote limestone gorge on Mallorca, a sun-baked Mediterranean island off the coast of Spain. He was investigating the possibility that a certain toad—thought to have been extinct for thousands of years—still lived.

He had found an extinct toad that clearly wasn't extinct.

Mayol had found tadpoles in the pools of a fast-moving stream, but he needed to see adults to know for sure what species they were. He waited excitedly for nightfall, and that's when he first heard the toad's call: a sharp *tink, tink, tink,* like the sound of a tiny hammer hitting metal. Following the calls, Mayol scaled a nearby cliff where he found the adults, each small enough to sit comfortably on a quarter, hiding in the cracks of the rocks. He had found an extinct toad that clearly wasn't extinct.

The Mallorcan midwife toad caused great excitement in Europe; it had been 80 years since a new amphibian was discovered there. But the toad was gravely endangered: perhaps fewer than 100 adults remained. The good news is the species has benefited from one of the world's most successful amphibian conservation programs.

Known to locals as "ferreret"—little ironworker—the midwife toad lives a bizarre life. Its distinct call is easy to hear but adults are difficult to find because their days are spent singing away while buried in wet sand or mud. Only at night, when it's time to feed on insects and small mollusks, do they enter the above-ground world. Other behaviors are equally strange. When it's time to mate, females compete for males by engaging in violent wrestling matches. And it's the dad who later gets saddled with most of the child-care responsibilities. This includes wrapping a string of a dozen or so eggs around his back legs and carrying them around for a month until they hatch.

Joan Mayol descends into the Mallorcan midwife toad's secret world.

But perhaps the most unusual part of the midwife toad story is how they declined. Fossils and historical records suggest they were wiped out by hungry snakes and other predators introduced to Mallorca by ancient Romans some 2,000 years ago.

What would it take to bring them back from the brink of extinction? Mayol and other scientists began by studying the toads' habits, then looked for ways to expand the population by creating new habitat in areas with few predators. They modified old watering holes once used by sheep and other livestock. They planted vegetation over other potential breeding holes to prevent the water from evaporating. And they lined rock depressions with concrete so they would hold rainwater. All told, some 20 sites were created or modified.

Tucked neatly between their father's hind legs, a clutch of midwife toad eggs remains out of harm's way.

While this was going on, zoos in Europe were busy raising midwife toads from 20 individuals caught in 1985. Four years later, 76 captive-bred tadpoles were released into the new habitats. Since then, researchers have reintroduced some 4,400 toads—all carefully screened for disease.

Today, the Mallorcan midwife toad appears to be on its way to recovery. At last count, there were several thousand toads in some two dozen sites. Encouragingly, almost all the mature adults appear to be reproducing.

To ensure there is enough genetic diversity for long-term survival, scientists are now analyzing DNA taken from toads from different subpopulations. Researchers are also taking steps to prevent the introduction of disease, including a halt to further introduction of captive-bred toads. While there has been talk about building a captive-breeding facility on Mallorca, this may not be needed. As one biologist on the team puts it: "Provided there are no catastrophes such as widespread drought or disease outbreaks, and if the populations continue to be monitored and managed when needed, then the species should be secure."

∧ Known as the little ironworker because of its distinctive song, the midwife toad is a conservation success story.

GLOBAL WARNING?

The western toad is no pushover. Its range covers most of western North America, from Alaska to California. It's fairly large for a toad, at up to 5 inches (12.5 cm) long. The female may lay as many as 12,000 eggs at a time, for as many as 20 years. With its squat, warty body, it even looks indestructible—like the SUV of the amphibian world.

But even these rugged animals are now in peril, and they've helped bring scientists around to the idea that global climate change may be contributing to amphibian declines.

In the late 1970s, biologist Andrew Blaustein discovered huge numbers of western toad eggs dying high in the Cascade Mountains of Oregon. Yet there was no destruction of habitat, and no pollution. Some suggested it was common for populations to rise and fall, but Blaustein disagreed. "We saw millions of eggs dying in the field. That's not a natural fluctuation. That's mass death."

The main suspect is now thought to be UV rays from the sun, which encourage the spread of disease among eggs laid in clear, shallow water. Blaustein also found that so little snow falls in some years that western toads are left with *only* shallow water. This is thought to be happening more and more, as a result of global warming.

In the larger frog world, Blaustein and others know that no single cause is to blame for the declines. Pollution, depletion of the ozone layer, global warming, disease and other factors combine to create many problems that may affect other life forms as well. If they're right, saving frogs will be more difficult—and more important.

Even tough guys like the western toad are disappearing, a sign to scientists that something   > more serious is afoot.

WHY SAVE FROGS?

There was a time when almost every child could walk to a stream, catch tadpoles and watch the miracle of metamorphosis unfold. Those days are fast disappearing. But would the world be any worse off without frogs? Conservationists are often asked that question, and they're quick to answer yes.

Frogs play an important role in nature. Because eggs and tadpoles are vulnerable, many frog species survive by laying as many eggs as possible. This provides a feast for a long list of predators. Eggs laid in water are a tasty treat for fish, while insects, birds and snakes prey on eggs laid on land—in fact, some snakes in Australia eat nothing but frogs. Insect larvae, birds and fish eat tadpoles. Adult frogs are good grub for bears, raccoons, minks, coyotes and other mammals. Without frogs, many of these predators would suffer.

Frogs have an impact at the other end of the food chain as well. In the days when insect-eating frogs were heavily harvested in India, for example, rice farmers had to rely on pesticides to control bugs. Frogs are a vital link between insects and large predators, one thread that holds together the web of life.

On a more selfish note, humans may want to save frogs for their own benefit. Researchers are only now beginning to discover the value of the chemicals produced by frogs. An effective painkiller has been derived from the skin glands of a poison dart frog in Ecuador. Other chemicals may one day provide humans with useful products ranging from mosquito repellent to surgical glue.

< A nutritious clutch of red-eyed leaf frog eggs serves as a juicy reminder of the vital role frogs play in natural ecosystems.

THE FUTURE FOR FROGS

For the gastric brooding frogs of Australia and the golden toads of Costa Rica, there is little hope. Barring the miraculous discovery of some overlooked population, these frogs will never be seen again. For a rapidly growing number of other species, the same is also true.

But humans haven't given up on frogs.

More than a third of all known frogs have been discovered since 1985.

Since people first realized that amphibians are in worldwide decline, interest in frogs has risen dramatically. Species that nobody knew existed are being found by the hundreds; more than a third of all known frog species have been discovered since 1985.

At the same time, cooperation between scientists has resulted in a better understanding of amphibian declines. Many questions remain, of course, but conservationists are ready to start turning the tide. Some solutions may be as simple as being more careful about when and where we spray pesticides, or how we ship frogs from place to place. Others, like reducing global warming and the seemingly endless human hunger for land and resources, may require wholesale changes in our behavior.

None of these goals will be attainable if humans don't care about frogs. The challenge for conservationists will be to convince people that these animals are every bit as fascinating and precious as pandas and whales, and to remind us all about the danger of doing nothing.

For the sake of frogs, let's hope they succeed.

FAST FACTS

Scientific names	• approximately 4,900 known species, making up 29 families in the amphibian order Anura
Size	• species range from the gold frog, at less than ⅜ of an inch (1 cm) long, to the goliath frog, with a maximum length of 12 inches (30 cm) and weight of more than 7 pounds (3.3 kg)
Life span	• largely unknown for frogs in the wild; one common toad lived 36 years in captivity
Locomotion	• can have webbed feet for swimming, adhesive pads on fingers and toes for climbing, or claws for digging
	• frogs and toads have four digits on the front limbs and five on the back
	• "flying" frogs have webbed fingers and toes, enlarged hands and feet and skin flaps used like parachutes for gliding great distances
	• some frogs can hop 20 times their own body length
Reproduction	• every species has a distinct mating call which males use to attract females; mating can occur over periods of months, or during brief mass gatherings
	• many species lay only a few dozen eggs each year, others tens of thousands
	• eggs are usually abandoned immediately, though some species go to great lengths to make sure they hatch safely

∨ The European common frog experiences the most familiar of the frog family's varied life cycles.

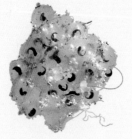

FROG SPAWN

external gills

RECENTLY HATCHED

internal gills

4 WEEKS OLD

Skin
- toads generally have rough, dry skin
- frogs usually have smooth, moist skin
- can vary from really tough to so thin that their internal organs can be seen through it

Senses
- can see in almost any direction, but only in black and white
- some species have a special eyelid that protects the eye while allowing in some light
- certain species hear their own calls, but not the calls of other species
- nose and eyes are on top of the head, allowing breathing and sight while mostly submerged
- adults and tadpoles can change skin color in response to danger or different light conditions

Diet
- most tadpoles eat algae
- most adult frogs eat insects, spiders, worms or slugs; some large species have been known to eat mice, birds and even other frogs

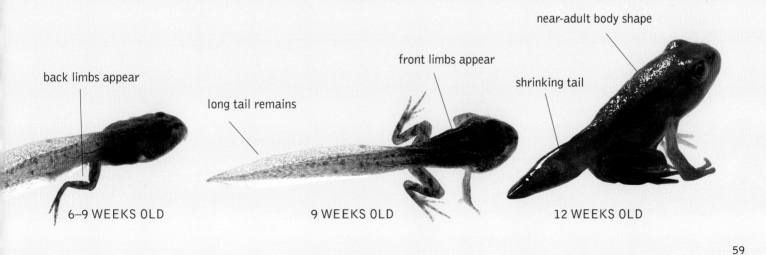

back limbs appear

long tail remains

front limbs appear

near-adult body shape

shrinking tail

6–9 WEEKS OLD

9 WEEKS OLD

12 WEEKS OLD

HOW YOU CAN HELP

If you would like to learn more about frogs or the projects designed to protect them, contact one of the following organizations or visit their websites:

Frogwatch USA
www.nwf.org/frogwatchUSA

c/o National Wildlife Federation, 11100 Wildlife Center Drive, Reston, VA, U.S.A. 20190–5362
Phone (703) 438-6000
Provides information on how to get involved in frog conservation, including activities such as counting frogs and building backyard ponds.

Frogwatch Canada
www.cnf.ca/frog

c/o Canadian Nature Federation, 1 Nicholas Street, Suite 606, Ottawa, Ontario, Canada KIN 7B7
Phone (613) 562-3447
Get directly involved in monitoring frog populations by joining this volunteer program.

North American Amphibian Monitoring Program
www.pwrc.usgs.gov/naamp

Patuxent Wildlife Research Center, 12100 Beech Forest Road, Suite 4039, Laurel, MD, U.S.A. 20708-4038
Phone (301) 497-5500
Help scientists monitor frog populations by participating in volunteer activities, such as frog-call surveys.

A Thousand Friends of Frogs
cgee.hamline.edu/frogs

c/o Center for Global Environmental Education,
Hamline University Graduate School of Education,
1536 Hewitt Avenue, St. Paul, MN, U.S.A. 55104-1284
Phone (651) 523-2480
Provides teachers and students with the latest news on frogs, and suggests activities involving frogs and conservation.

Amphibian Conservation Alliance
www.frogs.org

c/o Ashoka Foundation, 1700 North Moore Street, 20th Floor,
Arlington, VA, U.S.A. 22209
Phone (703) 807-5588
Features up-to-date research information and news from the frog world.

Amphibian Research Centre
frogs.org.au

P.O. Box 959, Merlynston 3058, Victoria, Australia
Phone: +61 (3) 9354 4718
Includes updates on the latest conservation efforts in Australia.

Canadian Amphibian and Reptile Conservation Network
www.carcnet.ca

Dedicated to understanding the threats affecting amphibians in Canada, as well as promoting conservation.

AmphibiaWeb
elib.cs.berkeley.edu/aw

Covers more than 1,000 species, including photos and sound files.

Declining Amphibian Populations Task Force
www.open.ac.uk/daptf

An international organization of scientists studying declining frog populations.

INDEX

PHOTO CREDITS

front cover: Royalty-free/Corbis/Magma
back cover: Rainer Schulte

p.2   Joe McDonald/Corbis/Magma
p.6   Konrad Wothe/Minden Pictures
p.10   Rainer Schulte
p.11   Michael & Patricia Fogden/Corbis/Magma
p.12   George McCarthy/Corbis/Magma
p.13, 15   Michael & Patricia Fogden/Minden Pictures
p.16, 17   courtesy of Alan Channing
p.18   Jonathan Blair/Corbis/Magma
p.19   David Wake
p.20   Michael & Patricia Fogden/Minden Pictures
p.21   Lee Berger
p.22, 23   Brian Harvey/AAP Image
p.24, 25   Alan Porritt/AAP Image
p.27   Andrew Meares/Sydney Morning Herald/Fairfax Photos
p.28   Mark Moffett/Minden Pictures
p.29   Stockfood/MaxxImages
p.30, 31   courtesy of Rainer Schulte
p.32, 33   courtesy of Mirza Dikari Kusrini
p.34   Bill Varie/Corbis/Magma
p.35–38   William Leonard/Vancouver Aquarium
p.39   Mark Moffett/Minden Pictures
p.40   Michael & Patricia Fogden/Minden Pictures
p.41   Joe McDonald/Corbis/Magma
p.42,43   courtesy of Pieter Johnson
p.44   Craig Line/AP Photo
p.45   Tim Fitzharris/Minden Pictures
p.46   Michael &Patricia Fogden/Minden Pictures
p.47   David A. Northcott/Corbis/Magma
p.49–51   courtesy of Joan Mayol
p.53   David A. Northcott/Corbis/Magma
p.54   Michael & Patricia Fogden/Minden Pictures
p.57   Tim Fitzharris/Minden Pictures
p.58–59   DK Images

AUTHOR'S NOTE

Thanks to the many people around the world who were generous enough to share their stories and offer their help: Lee Berger, Alan Channing, Claude Gascon, Richard Griffiths, Tim Halliday, Alex Hyatt, Pieter Johnson, Lee Kats, David Kizirian, Cathy Merriman, Mirza Dikari Kusrini, Gerry Marantelli, Joan Mayol, John Richardson, Rainer Schulte, Paul Speck, Simon Stuart, Michael Tyler and David Wake.

This book is for Ben.